novum pocket

Christine Stretton

Why Does The Floor Feel Further Away?

A Collection of Poetry

novum 📖 pocket

© 2023 novum publishing

ISBN 978-3-903382-26-8
Cover photo:
Jiri Kratochvil I Dreamstime.com
Cover design, layout & typesetting:
novum publishing

www.novum-publishing.co.uk

Climate neutral
Print product
ClimatePartner.com/16547-2201-1002

Contents

DEDICATION

I would like to thank my family, my son Simon and his wife Sharron. My daughter Rachael and her partner Jamie and his daughter Dakota, and especially my grandson, Jackson, who has not only kept me on my toes at times but has been a joy to be around. Even when he says things to his teacher like, "If an old woman comes to pick me up it's my grandma." The reply from me being, "If he survives the weekend, you will see him on Monday."

I would also really like to thank Gary Smith, whose meditation sessions opened up something within me that allowed the poems to come in. Chris Greenwood, who set up Angels Corner, and Adrian Mark Riley, also from Angels Corner. Rob and Liz Linden for welcoming me into their lovely team at Kickstart Wellness Center, and Sophie Fox, who I can meditate with again. Thank you to Adrian Baxter for opening the door for me and attuning me to be able to practice reiki. Last but not least I have to give a big thank you to my partner in crime, Linda Green, who has been a close friend for many years and has been on this journey with me but prefers to be behind the scenes.

INTRODUCTION

My name s Christine Stretton. I am a sixty-
nine-year-old mother of two
children, Simon and Rachael.
I am also blessed with a
nine-year-old grandson named Jackson.
I have lived alone ever since my partner,
Stuart, died in 2020.
I was brought up working class. My dad was an
electrician and mum was a weaver.
Both myself and my brother, David, were
brought up as Catholics and lived in Halifax,
West Yorkshire – where we still do – on the
outskirts. It is nothing like it was in the fifties.
The dark satanic mills were in full swing then
and created a sooty smog which clung to the
valley.
We both attended Catholic schools
and went to mass every Sunday.
However, when I was about fifteen I began a
hairdressing apprenticeship. I decided that my
heart was not in it and all I was doing
was going through the motions.
I stopped practising and got on with
no more thoughts of religion or God.
My brother also reached
the same conclusion later.

It was as I got older that I gave
it some thought. I never felt
like an atheist so wondered if
it had to be one or the other.
I have always been curious
and love reading, so I began
reading up on other religions,
especially Buddhism and the Sufis.
As I got older, I began wondering
whether there had to be more to this life.
If you just disappeared when you died,
what would the point of it be?

Along with a close friend,
we booked a session with a local psychic.
I was interested in having a Tarot
card reading. After the reading,
he suggested visiting a spiritual
centre in Brighouse, West Yorkshire,
called Still Waters, to see what
I thought about it.

I found a group that held
meditation sessions one evening
a week, run by a man named Gary Smith.
With his protection I felt safe
to go quite deep. I would visualise
myself in a lift beginning at floor
twenty and going down.
Then it was seeing where you
were when the lift doors opened.
Sometimes I think I fell asleep
because his voice would fade away
and when we were brought back around,
I had no idea where I had been.

It was around this time that
I began to get one or two verses of
poems and write them down.

Quite a few years ago, Still Waters closed down
very abruptly, so that was the end of those
meditation sessions. I find it more distracting
to meditate at home. Boo Boo would bark or the
phone would ring so I could never go as deep.

A few years later, one of the mediums we met
at Still Waters, called Chris Greenwood, felt
she ought to begin her own open circle. This
is a group in which people who are psychic
or are drawn to it can develop. This spiritual
group is called Angels Corner. We do not have
a permanent centre so have used various
different venues, usually a room in a pub. At the
moment, we are lucky to have the use of a
café one evening a week.
I have not developed into mediumship skills but
found I was more drawn to healing.

A lot of the time I began to get one
or two verses of poems in my mind, usually
while I was in the local woods walking my dog
Tallulah, Boo Boo for short.
It did feel like they just popped in unexpectedly.
I have since found out this can
also be known as channelling.
An example of this is part of a poem I received
one day which was, "The only thing that
matters is today, fretting about the past and
fears about your future.

"Takes your moment in the here and now and steals it clean away." (Poem: Seize the moment.) So as soon as we got home, I scribbled it down, then more of it followed.

Sometimes parts of poems came in my mind at inconvenient moments, such as in the dawn of the morning. Thinking I would lose them, I would hurriedly copy them down. I did find out that that was not the case though, so I just pop them down when it is convenient for me.
I was bought a lovely spiral-bound book in which to copy them but found I had filled that, so I bought another, which is also filled. So I had another poetry book as a Christmas present. I began to realise that the poetry was teaching me things or helping me through difficult situations, so I began to think it was selfish just to read them out at Angels Corner or on Facebook. A few people also told me they should be shared more widely.

As a result, I decided that they should be published.

I also began an apprenticeship in reiki, in a place in Elland known as Xanadu, with a reiki master called Adrian Baxter. Over time, I completed my reiki one and two attunements.
However, Adrian retired
and Xanadu closed down.

Another reiki practitioner, Adrian Mark Riley, whom we first met at Still Waters, is also part of our group at Angels Corner. He has passed his master teacher level and is therefore providing another apprenticeship, so I can continue.

I have also found another Wellness Centre that do have their own base just up the road from where I live, run by Rob and Liz Linden. They also have reiki shares once a month, which I enjoy taking part in. A reiki share is when we give healing to each other instead of clients.

A lady called Sophie Fox provides angelic meditations once a month, so I have been really lucky to be able to continue on this path, which poetry is a part of.

A BOAT CALLED DESTINY

Floating down the river on
my boat called Destiny,
It is like a lazy river with no
motor or oars needed, just a rudder.
I can see streams leading off from both sides,
I float past the one where
I can make lots of money,
I am not greedy.
The one where I am being waved at
from people on fancy yachts,
I am not envious, so I don't feel needy.
Then there is one that makes me shudder,
I can hear raised voices saying things like,
"It's all your fault,"
"No, it's not, it's yours,
I will never speak to you again,
I will never forgive you for this."
I prefer to keep on floating past,
this is one river I'd rather miss.
Then I see a lovely one and hear,
"Come down here,
the world owes you a living,
Fill yourself up with Mother
Earth's milk and honey."
I do not think so; how awful to think you
can take without giving.

Then there is the stream
whose banks are not so pretty,
I hear, "Come down and rest up,
you poor thing, fancy being stuck
on your boat all alone."
I ask what is the name of this stream.
"Why, it's self-pity."
"No, thank you, I'm fine."
But there is a stream
I keep finding difficult to avoid,
time after time.
I hear, "Hey, where do you
think you are going?"
I reply, "I do not know
but I'm enjoying the ride."
"Don't be stupid;
what happens if you spring
a leak or hit a sand bank?"
"Come here; you need my help.
I will get some oars and
then do the rowing."
Yes, this stream is my own ego.
I will keep trying to allow
my boat to take its own course,
All the while trying to ignore
my pesky companion by my side.

A CARAVAN HOME

Sat here in our static caravan,
I marvel at the magic that
has brought this about.
It seemed to happen so quickly,
I felt at times if only I had known.
My grandson's request for one
seemed such a lovely dream.
I thought it would take a
lottery win to fulfil.
So I added his request to my
list of affirmations,
To be later on in the future,
or so it would seem.
However, guided by
synchronicity to a couple
who had just bought a second-hand
one much more reasonable.
Our touring caravan had
already been on a campsite
near Bridlington for three years.
The company had eight
other sites and if we found one
on their other sites,
They would move it for free,
and part-exchange our own caravan.
Curiosity led me to go online
and have a peep, but still having a few fears.

As it was the school holidays we took
our grandson to look at one costing twelve
thousand pounds.
He loved it, as he would have his
own bedroom and was such an excited little boy.
I was worried, even with my affirmation,
but popped a one-thousand-pound deposit on it.
In order to make this happen we
had to find a ploy.
Then we had a phone call and letter telling us
we could have more equity release.
It then took a long time to get a
surveyor to revalue our house,
This was causing me a lot of stress
and a real test of faith.
Could we actually pull this off,
or would it end in tears?
But the other side knows what it is doing,
It all went ahead okay in time for our grandson
to stay in it for half-term.
Then my affirmation was even more magic,
Not only was there was enough
money to pay for the caravan
But also a balcony.
Manifestation is available for everyone;
just thank the Universe for what you wish for.
If it can happen for you and well as me.

A MESSAGE TO THE YOUNGER GENERATION

It is easy to go with the general feeling that it is
the older generation who are leaving you with a
planet that is in a mess,
That we had it easy,
we could buy houses and cars,
As for our environment we couldn't care less.
However for thousands of
us that wasn't the case,
We were the sixties generation
who were changing the world,
We were bringing in colour,
as the world had felt beige,
We had make love not war and flower power,
Psychedelic music and meditation,
yes, there were also mind-bending drugs,
But we really felt that we were making
a big difference, groovy not square,
We felt that this was our time and our hour.
Then the National Front began raising its head,
So we countered with Rock Against Racism,
Thousands of us meeting in a
big city, marching for hours,
Shouting smash the National Front. We wanted
a multi-cultural society instead.

Admittedly we also had brilliant bands,
playing for free. The Police in Leeds,
Steel Pulse in Manchester, and Toyah in
Brixton, and always the
Buzzcocks as back up for lead.
Then some countries began an arms race,
the thinking being,
To keep their own country safe
they had to have more nuclear warheads.
That made no sense to a lot of us, remembering
the fate of Nagasaki and Hiroshima.
So we joined CND, Ban The Bomb,
there were also a lot of women
gathered together on Greenham
Common for a long time to protest
against American Cruise Missiles placed there.
Singing songs and holding hands
to create a human chain.
Smokeless zones were brought in to
remove the smog, but the fallout
from that was acid rain.
We did have plenty of jobs still available
and houses were cheap, making it
much easier to Own your own home.

But a cold wind of change was slowly
creeping in now called Thatcherism,
suddenly council tenants could buy
their houses at the same time
that the thinking became there
was money in Property.
So the cheap ones were bought by
property developers; the age of
affordable housing had Been and gone.
So we now had the chance to
have more social mobility.
It became important to have the latest wares,
So along came more HP, if it is broken,
throw it out, no more need for repairs.
There is plenty where that came from
and now we have the ability.
Before we realised, we now had huge
corporations who held the power,
Their mantra as always is we have
to have growth, so they persuaded
people they had to have the latest gadget,
happiness lay with the latest must-have.
For Mother Earth this is not our finest hour.
Even when the scientists warned
them about global warming, they tried
to ignore it and Keep their own stability.

Now agreeing to hold summits, this has
had the effect of kicking the can
further down the road.
They have a plan to cut omissions,
which is a step forward,
But they still want to be rich before
they get too old.
It felt like all our hopes and dreams of a
fair and safe future for all of us had
been consigned to history's dustbin.
So please, before you look to all
our generation to place the blame,
Research some of our inspiration, listen to
Martin Luther's I have a dream speech,
George Harrison, John Lennon's
Give Peace a Chance, but especially the
words of his beautiful song, Imagine.
Yes, it appeared we lost our cause back then, but
with your generation's new passion
to save Mother Earth, it's wonderful
to see it return yet again.
This time I have far more hope it will work,
as it feels like a warmer wind blowing,
While you walk on her turf.

A PLEA FROM MOTHER EARTH

I am your Mother Earth,
providing everything you need,
I give you air to breathe and water
to drink and grow your food.
I love every living thing that on
my surface does dwell,
But sadly, at the moment
I am being more damaged
By people who have in
their hearts only greed.
I know to live it is important
to have some money,
But my future lies in the
hands of big corporations
Who want all my milk and honey.
They grab anything they can
using even bribery and corruption,
Of my wellbeing or the likes of
you and yours they have no care.

A PLEA

Mother Earth is in transition,
The darkness versus the light.
There are many of you who chose this mission,
To help join in the fight.
Help us lift Mother Earth's vibration
Out of negativity and fear.
As you become more enlightened,
You will feel love and joy draw near.
All it takes is a simple prayer each day,
To request the Divine White light to shine,
In all the darkest places and in
all the darkest hearts.
One single candle burning in a dark room
Helps push back the night.
Thousands of candles burning,
Give far more power and might.

A SHINING DIAMOND

Visualise your soul as a diamond which
is made up of different facets,
A pure soul will be the most brilliant.
However, collecting karma through many lives,
forms like a black sludge,
This sticks to certain facets dulling the shine.
So those brave souls who can be resilient,
Choose to come back again,
as many times as they need,
Face their problems usually one by one,
It could be that with certain people,
you bear a grudge,
You are maybe trying to overcome a
lack of patience or greed.
It takes far longer to achieve this on spirit side,
where no negativity exists,
As your every wish is manifest immediately.
Eventually your soul will become
restless and feel the need to progress.
Just as staying in the same class
at school year after year.
By returning to Mother Earth,
she can provide you with every situation

For you to overcome, it is not the lesson
but how you deal with it,
Whether it is with strangers or
those we hold most dear.
So like a fast pass at a theme park,
you can speed up the process.
If you keep bumping into the
same problem time after time,
It is probably your soul nudging
you to get out that polish,
Give that facet a shine.

A VERY BRITISH SUMMER HOLIDAY

Looking forward to a very
British summer holiday,
It will be such a relief after all
the months of lockdown,
To get the opportunity to go away.
We are so lucky to have a
caravan in Bridlington,
Sat there biding its time,
waiting for us to return.
Getting the go ahead from
The Flower of May,
To tell us we can go back,
As we are already in July,
it's deciding what to pack.
This is not easy, as I will need
summer clothes and sandals,
Suntan cream so we don't burn.
But also a jumper, wellies and a mac.
But to be able to stand on that
cliff top looking out to sea,
It will be sad without my partner,
But still so lovely to be back.

BIG FAT LIES

Does anyone remember as a child,
That no matter what it was you had done,
Being told that lying about it made it far worse?
If you were caught lying it was
much more trouble you were in.
But it appears this no longer holds true,
Our leaders feel it perfectly okay to
cover their tracks with lies and spin.
President Trump for one is truth averse,
As for our own leaders,
thinking we are easily taken in.
Hoping we will either believe,
or forget their lies,
Such as Dominic Cummings
breaking lockdown,
Then telling us he drove so
far to test his eyes.
It makes me sad that this is
an era of post-truth,
Honesty should be seen as
something to be cherished,
Instead of it being a curse.

BUS PASS

After half past nine I can hop on
a bus and go anywhere,
Now I have my free bus pass.
After failing my driving test four times,
Not being able to afford to keep going.
Now it feels like I have more freedom,
As I do not have to worry about the bus fare.
It also means more people on the
buses leads to fewer cars on the road.
It's good they are getting busier with
less empty seats to spare.
The bus etiquette is still in place,
after paying or swiping,
Do not look directly at the
other passengers' faces,
Find an empty seat or sit next to
someone of your own sex.
If somebody drunk gets on,
hope they sit in another space.
Most passengers are looking
down at their mobile phones,
So at times it feels like you have
boarded the Zombie Express.
But I still like to look out of the window.

But just as on a plane most
passengers could not care less.
Car drivers sat alongside us at the lights,
Feel their car is completely private.
Not wishing to be nosey,
but they are within your sights.
Nine times out of ten they
are picking their nose.
I have roped in my grandson and our dog.
He likes to go upstairs and sit at the front,
She is a bit nervous and gets off
far more eagerly than on.
I am so glad that the bus pass is
still one of our rights.

CARING ABOUT MOTHER EARTH

Mother Earth does need her warriors in
order to slow down the destruction.
Banging on the door of the Establishment
With their message to stop damaging
our planet just for short-term gain.
A lot of people find their behaviour annoying,
causing too much disruption.
But groups such as Green Peace and
Extinction Rebellion do have their place.
She also needs people working behind
the scenes who quietly care,
Not needing to show their faces.
There is also recycling, using less plastic
and eating either less or no meat.
It is the realisation that
continuous growth and profit
Is something Mother Earth cannot sustain.
Cutting down or burning the rainforest
in order to grow more palm oil,
Will eventually lead to a desert,
as there will be no rain.

More of our animals will be made homeless
and therefore will become extinct.
She also needs people to send her their love,
respect and healing.
Losing more of our green spaces in favour of
buildings and concrete,
Leaves us with a very depressed feeling,
As it is within Mother Nature
and her beauty spots
That makes our spirits feel replete.
She needs people to care in whatever
way feels right for them.
Unlike the unaware and greedy people,
It is looking ahead with knowledge that we
cannot eat gold or drink oil.

CHAIN REACTION

The term "a little kindness" goes a
long way is quite true,
It could be something as simple as
giving another person a smile,
Or remembering to say thank you.
It may just restore that person's
faith in humanity,
And brighten up their day.
They then may go on to smile
at the next person,
You have set up a chain reaction.
However, due to modern living with
all its rushing and stress,
Can give some people a difficult life.
No time to stop let alone smile,
The world is full of trouble and strife.
It could be in your rush you lost
your temper with another driver,
Choosing to beep your horn
and swear and shout.
He might then go home and take
it out on his wife.
You have set up a chain reaction.
Like throwing a stone into a pond,
the ripples keep moving out.

CHILHOOD SAYINGS

Isn't it funny how the sayings adults
told you in your childhood
Stay in your mind up to present day?
Some have proved useful, while others,
you wish you could forget them if you could.
If I told my mum I could not do
something, she would say,
"There is no such word as 'can't'."
That one has been useful to me,
as I had to try another way,
So if plan A failed, try plan B.
One of Mum's I felt was a bit mean,
If I hurt myself, she would say,
"You will die after it,"
As she applied the Germolene.
When I worriedly asked why,
her reply would be, "You can't die before it."
I still find myself repeating some of them,
such as if I am putting something off,
Saying to myself, this will not buy
the baby a new bonnet.
Grandma had her sayings too, such as,
"Ne'er cast a clout til May is out."
This translated as, until the first of June,
I would have to wear a coat and hat.

Another was if I pulled a silly face,
I would be told, "If the wind changed,
my face would stay like that."
But it was my dad's that really
muddled my head,
If I asked him, "Why?" he would answer, "Z."
If I asked him where he was going,
he would reply,
"There and back to see how far it is."
If I asked him how much
something cost he would say,
"Money in fair words."
Then the old chestnut if my
brother and I were noisy,
"Children should be seen and not heard."
But the one that puzzled me the
most was if I said, "But Dad, I thought –"
He always said, "You know what thought did."
Pondering on this for a while I asked him,
"Dad, what did thought do?"
To be told, "It followed a cart load of
poo and thought it was a wedding."

CHILDHOOD SAYINGS TWO

I wonder if this is one of the reasons
why our generation were more naïve
Compared to the children of today.
We found adult conversations
boring, so quickly left,
Off we would go and out to play.
But there were two more sayings that
I was given when I had children of my own.
My auntie's was, "You cannot put an
old head onto young shoulders."
Another of my mum's was,
"Allow children to be children,
They will have most of their
lives with adult problems.
All too soon their
childhood will be gone."

EVERYDAY MIRACLES

A beautiful sunny autumn day
in North Dean Wood,
Me and the pooch strolling
along and feeling good.
Admiring the odd leaf reflecting
the sun falling down from the trees,
I thanked the Universe for
moments like these.

When I heard a rustle behind my back,
Turning around to look down the track,
I saw every tree drop lots of leaves,
falling down like golden rain.
Two minutes later the show was over, but the
memory of it will always remain.

No wind was blowing on that beautiful morn,
I know I was allowed to see a small miracle,
Making me glad that I was born.

FASCINATING ANGEL NUMBERS

Now we are in 2020 I feel it could
be a special and auspicious year,
It has dawned on me that this year
the number six figures loud and clear.
So from the shelf I reached
for my *Angels' Numbers* book.
To begin with I looked up
the number twenty.
Twenty, it reads, your
connection to spirit is strong.
Fill your heart and mind with faith right now.
I was so intrigued by the number six,
I took a closer look.
To begin with, my grandson is age six;
our house number is number six,
along with our caravan site, which is H6.
Six, it reads, do not worry or
obsess about material things.
Worry lessens the effectiveness of prayers.
Fortunately, the angels can answer
your prayers if you ask them to.
The next number is sixty, which
my friend will become this year.
Sixty, it reads, you are in between
focusing on the spirit and material world.

This number wants you to balance
your focus and remember spirit is
the force behind everything in your life.
The next number is sixty-six, the age I am now;
what a coincidence in every way.
Sixty-six, it reads, burdening myself
with worries and stress makes it harder
for me to hear my angels' loving help.
I need to spend more time in prayer and
meditation and open my arms to receive it.
Now, the amount of sixes we have here,
you have guessed it, is six.
So, using the times table, six sixes are thirty-six.
Thirty-six, it reads, the Ascended Masters
ask us to keep our thoughts focused on spirit,
releasing any material worries to them.
This final message ties in with all
others in a serendipitous way.
I have a good feeling about this year;
I think it will be sprinkled with some
special angel magic.

FEAR IS INFLEXIBLE

Fear is inflexible; in extreme it can hold
us back and keep us rooted to the spot.
It is a normal human emotion
that can be useful at times,
But allowing it to take over and rule
our lives is not a good plan,
As it certainly will not.
It is easier said than done,
but when you keep feeling fear,
Give it over to a higher power.
This is the unconditional love
that surrounds us, always near.
It is not an old man with a long white beard
playing God in an ivory tower
But a force that not only keeps us safe
but also those we hold dear.

GO AHEAD AND THINK BIG AND BE BOLD

As well as unconditional love, the Universe
knows only abundance,
If what you wish for is for the greater good,
Just ask and believe.
What we have been led to believe is full of words
twisted to become a falsehood.
For instance, we were told, "Thou shall not
want", which could mean it was wrong
to ask for anything.
The real meaning is, "Thou shall not
want for anything, so asking is not a sin."
The idea that scarcity and being poor
makes a person more devout
Is perpetrated by people who want to
keep the lion's share,
As they think it gives them power.
Just ask and believe.
So, dare to dream, visualise
what it is you want,
As long as it does no harm to
other people, or Mother Earth,
It is already yours to have and to hold.
You are the ones with the power,
As you have the Universe behind you,
So go ahead think big and be bold.

HAPPY MEDIUM

I always prefer a happy medium,
nothing too extreme or passive,
In fact, the middle way.
Nothing is either all black or all white,
Looking from both points of view,
the best reasoning
Is usually in the middle, which is grey.
Two people arguing with all their might,
Busy putting across their own point of view,
Not listening to one another,
because they are both right.
The truth is probably down the middle.
Spending all your time working
and chasing after wealth,
You will not have enough spare time to enjoy it,
Try and find a balance, enough to be
comfortable but also to have some fun.
Spending lots of time pounding
pavements, or in the gym,
Worrying about your body size or health
Has its place; trying to look after
yourself is not a sin,
But remember to give yourself some time out,
Chill out or meditate, do things you enjoy,
Find time in your busy day.

So, I try to look for a happy medium in all
things, follow that middle way.
It is not always easy, as some people
think I am being too passive,
Trying not to get too drawn into
other people's dramas,
Makes my life easier, so for me it does pay.

HOLD YOUR NERVE

As Mother Earth moves further into her shift,
You can feel the quickening,
It feels like the climate has gone mad.
Natural disasters such as
earthquakes and hurricanes
Will be larger and more destructive.
A lot of people are thinking
these times are really bad.
This is a call to all her light workers,
There will be a growth of fear and despair,
But Mother Earth needs you to
stay positive and stand firm.
Hold your head up high while sending out
A healing prayer.
Time is speeding up at a faster rate,
A year feels like ten months
and ten hours in a day.
For you light workers it will feel
like a bumpy ride,
But keep your nerve and hold on tight,
In these dark times it is your job
to be a beacon of light.
Help speed Mother Earth on her way,
After everything she has had to put up with,
It is what she deserves.
As for you light workers, your reward will be
much happier times ahead,
We need to ensure that we will win the day.

INTENTIONS

As you step out of your old overcoat and
prepare to go to your real home,
Your Spirit will feel as light as air.
You will be your real self,
as your ego will also be gone.
As you go through your life review you will see
It was your intentions behind
your actions that will be laid bare.
No place for excuses or prevarications,
Were your intentions for the greater good,
Or were they self-serving?
Such as a rich person donating
lots of money to charity
Purely to avoid extra taxes
Will mean nothing to the spiritual lore.
However, a poorer person giving j
ust one pound to a homeless person,
Because they feel empathy,
counts so much more.
If things do not always turn
out the way we hoped,
And it feels it all went wrong,
You have not screwed up if you
had the right intentions.

LAW OF THE LAND

So, the law of this land
allows for corporate thieves,
In fact, rewards them by
bestowing titles on them.
Allowing them to do as they please.
(Sir) Philip Green has been allowed
to sail away on his fancy yacht,
Enjoying a Playboy lifestyle,
While leaving behind thousands
of decent working people on their knees.
Laughing as he spends their pension pot.
Most feel he should be stripped of his assets,
Not out of envy, as swapping with
someone so heartless, we would not.
No, it should be given back to the workers,
But no, he can go and play on Mustique,
While they will be branded shirkers.
The majority of people in this land would
benefit from a law being passed
That would make this practice illegal.
But it would struggle to
get through the Commons,
And would definitely be thrown
out of the House of Lords.
So, it's just a case of,
"Oh that naughty Sir Philip Green,
He's managed to pull off another jolly wheeze."

LOVE COMES IN MANY GUISES

Love comes in many guises.
Looking for that one true love, who will be
your soulmate as well as your best friend,
Some people turn to online dating,
looking on sites such as Tinder.
You may be lucky and find that special person,
whose love for you will never end.
Or end up with a passionate fling that
is short-lived, ending up with a cinder.
We love our children and grandchildren and
they love us, as well as toys and sweets.
So, as well as looking after them we love to buy
them treats, being proud of their achievements
and providing the odd surprise.
We love our pets and wish we could keep their
unconditional love longer
than a few short years,
It always feels too early when they leave us,
and their little souls cross over Rainbow Bridge,
Leaving us feeling empty with lots
of sadness and tears,

But we will find the greatest love of all,
for when our work on Earth is done,
We will shed our bodies like an old overcoat,
rising up and away,
Enveloped in such unconditional love
that it will feel like bliss.
It will be then that we will realise our journey
home in spirit has once again begun.

NOVEMBER FOG

Stepping out this morning into a November fog,
The horizon has disappeared,
making the land and sky become one.
There is a pool of colour wherever
you happen to be,
But behind you as you walk it closes behind you,
Like curtains being drawn when the day is done.
Opening up in front of you,
allowing you a little way to see.
Unlike a sea fret, where it is like
misty fingers swirling around,
Rather, this feels like a blanket
thrown over the sky,
Muting sounds as well as colour,
as you make your way home.

ONE DAY AT A TIME

How brilliant that the people of this nation
Adjusted so quickly to social
distancing and isolation.
The hardest part being unable to
have our family and friends around,
As the world turned upside down.
For grandparents it is not being with
our grandchildren that we missed,
Thank goodness for phones,
Facebook and WhatsApp,
But they can never replace that cuddle and kiss.
For people in isolation that are all alone,
Their houses could begin to feel like prison,
Instead of home.
Those people worried about
their financial situation,
Causing them sleepless nights and stress.
Those people on the front line working all
hours, both day and night,
Wondering if a break for them
willould ever be in sight.
So, I request the people in the
media and the press,
To bear in mind all the people under duress.
It's time for them to change
the way they give the news,

To cut out sensationalism and
tone it down a bit.
We are a captive audience so you
have nothing to lose.
As far as some of the wilder predictions of it
lasting months or years,
Stick that where the sun does not shine.
Respect the fact that for our own mental health,
We are trying to get through this situation,
one day at a time.
Go back to reviewing it every three weeks,
make it easier to cope with,
So most of us will come out fine.

PANIC

I do recall in the 1970s the
threat of a nuclear strike,
There would be a four-minute warning.
The advice was, in that time to
remove all your inside doors,
Place them around your dining table,
make a den,
Pray the bomb does not fall.
I am not one to panic,
but I would not even have
found a screwdriver,
Let alone have removed one door.
Looking back now it seems so stupid,
no need to panic at all.

Along came 1999 – we were told that computers
would not be able to work
In the switch over to the year 2000.
So, at the stroke of midnight
there would be a blackout.
Planes would fall out of the sky,
Hospital equipment would fail.
Patients would die.
The whole country would crash and burn.
Other people calmly got on with
their New Year celebrations,

A possible hangover had been all,
no need to panic at all.
Along came 2012, leading up to Christmas,
It seems thousands of years ago, a very clever
civilisation called the Mayans
Had a calendar that ended on 12, 12, 2012.
This had to herald the end of the world.
Let's gather our families around
us and stay in our own homes.
The sun rose as usual on the thirteenth,
Quick, let's get on with Christmas,
off to the mall.
No need to panic at all.

2019 has brought the spectre of "No Brexit",
The usual rhetoric has been rolled out.
Maybe we will find there is no
need to panic at all.

PEOPLE ARE NOT POSSESSIONS

People are not possessions like
house furniture or a car,
We see too many people who
think their partners they do own,
For us we feel that is wrong by far.
If you feel you need another person
to make you whole,
Then it's time to look deeper inside yourself.
You always have been a whole person
because you possess a soul.
We keep hearing, "I do not want to
be left on the shelf."
First learn to love yourself as you are,
Stop beating yourself up;
anyone can make a mistake.
Happy, confident people always
attract people to them,
Two whole people loving each
other is like the icing on a cake.
Far less trouble and strife,
Much more give and take.
Your children too are just on loan,
To be entrusted with them is a great honour.
Please nurture them and provide a loving home.
Give them fair discipline and try to be a good
example every day.

Avoid making it your dreams
you wish them to fulfil.
Allow them to leave home with
confidence and go their own way,
That way you respect their own free will.

POO BAGS IN MY POCKET

Whatever jacket or coat I choose
I find poo bags in my pocket.
This happens a lot to those
whose walking companion
Has four legs instead of two.
Even at the caravan my days are planned
By where Boo and I will go that day,
It could be the beach or Danes Dyke.
Wherever we go it's more of a stroll,
We are not up for a hike.
No matter if it is sunshine, rain or snow,
With her at my side we sally
forth into the fresh air.
Witnessing the change of seasons,
Chatting away to strangers,
as well as people we know.
I hope I have many more seasons where
I find poo bags in my pocket,
With my faithful pooch walking by my side.
Dogs are such good companions
for several different reasons,
But mainly the love in those trusting eyes.

POPPING IN

A loved one popped into my dream last night,
It's always a special treat
which fills me with delight.
Some have passed to the other side,
While others have found me in their sleep.
You always know it was a real visit,
As the memory of it does not fade
with the morning light.
I am always frustrated with myself,
as I always ask them if they are all right,
I could kick myself – why didn't I ask them
something more profound,
Which could give me more insight?
I wonder if it is the surprise and
joy of seeing them again,
Popping in and what feels like far too quickly,
Disappearing out of sight.

RAINBOW RACE

When you see a rainbow
hanging there in the sky,
It lifts your spirits, as it's such a lovely sight.
The colours sit side by side perfectly
in order to form a bow.
Not one colour dominates the other,
as they all have their part to play,
In order to make a whole.
It was supposed to be the same
for the human race.
Not one colour dominating the other,
as they all have their part to play,
In order to make a whole.
It should not matter if you are black,
brown, yellow, red or white.
It is both ignorant and depressing
that people are still being singled out
Just by the colour of their skin.
A step in the right direction would
be if parents and grandparents,
No matter what colour or creed,
stopped passing on any prejudice,
Instead, teaching them it is more
important to recognise the soul within.

RECIPE FOR A HAPPY CHILDHOOD

LASHINGS OF LOVE

It is important the child feels loved by the
significant adults in their life.
To pick them up each time they fall,
Comfort them when they are ill,
Give them the confidence to walk tall.

SCOOPFULS OF SECURITY
Providing them with a safe and loving home,
Giving them a routine, although once in
place it can be flexible.
Regular meals, clean clothes and a
space to call their own.

BUCKETFULS OF BOUNDARIES

This allows the child to feel safe when
beginning to explore their world.
An adult to provide a watchful eye,
Being told what is safe to touch,
Pointing out dangers while
explaining to them why.

A MASSIVE HELPING OF MAGIC

Childhood is only a short thirteen years,

It is important to give them a
lot of happy memories.
Sometimes it isn't easy with
tantrums and tears.

MIX IT ALTOGETHER

Show them the magic of nature,
Provide them with a plant to plant,
Allow them to run, skip and bound,
Along with the time to watch an ant.
Lots of exploring, laughter and fun,
Bubble baths, singing and dancing.

When as an adult at times life
can become humdrum,
You can look back at your childhood
and remember there is still magic around.

REMEMBER

Remember this simple poetry
is sent from above,
The message we send is one of love.
When problems cause you worry and fear,
We are just a whisper away, always near.

You chose this path before you came,
With all the ups and downs, joys and sorrows.
Your spirit gains strength, overcoming pain,
But remember there is also laughter and joys
In your tomorrows.

SEARCHING

For many years now I have been reading
lots of books of an esoteric nature,
Books written by mediums, about angels,
star systems and reincarnation,
To name just a few.
My bookshelves are overflowing,
and I look forward to reading them with delight.
Some I was not so sure of,
as for me they did not ring quite true.
I ordered myself a new one for my birthday,
From Amazon's extensive library
with older books as well as new.
This book is called *messages from Jesus
and the Celestials v1*.
The first edition was published in 1940,
channelled by a medium named
James E. Padgett, with help from a
man known as Leslie R. Stone.
In 1914, James, using automatic writing,
channelled a message claiming to
be from Jesus of the bible,
He doubted the message so much
that into the bin he threw it.
However, his beloved wife Mary and his mother
and father, all spirit side,

Gave messages to him, telling him to stop
doubting himself and have faith,
As the message from Jesus was true.
He then kept all the messages he had
written down from Jesus,
the Celestials, and his family.
Jesus sent the messages to inform us that the
interpretations of his words in the bible
Had been misunderstood
and therefore were wrong.
He came to Earth to show us his example
of the Way, the Truth and the Light.
Not to be worshipped, but for us to also pray to
Our Father for His divine love to enter our soul.
He did not die to take on our sins
but purely from men's fear.
Our soul's progression to each i
ndividual does belong.
Spirit side holds many spheres;
a person's soul goes where it has earned,
Along with other souls who have
reached the same development.
This includes the lower spheres,
where they can continue to carry out
Evil and bad deeds if they so choose.

However, no soul is stuck, once it
decides to look for enlightenment,
It can be raised up, no matter
how the others may scream and shout.
Souls destined for the higher spheres find
themselves in a place of extraordinary beauty
With like-minded souls who
are filled with happiness.
This was where James's beloved wife
was when he received her messages.
She followed Jesus's advice and prayed
to the Father for His divine love,
Then found herself raised up
into the celestial spheres,
She informed James that she was now
not just happy but filled with bliss.

SEND HEALING

It is understandable that a lot of people
are sick of war and pray for peace,
However, it would be far better
instead to send out healing.
The reason for this is that war and
peace are part of the same vibration.
Think of it like a seesaw: in the
middle you would find arms dealing.
Everybody can do this; you do
not need any training,
What counts is the good
intentions behind the feeling.
So it is far better to avoid sending your
energy through prayers and supplication
In order to lessen the liking for conflict,
Send your thoughts towards a healing vibration.

SHOPPING IN A FOG

Nipping to the shop now feels so different,
First of all not only remembering your
bags for life as well as your bank card
But now having to remember your mask.
Having to pop it on at the door
causes your glasses to steam up,
Then finding yourself in a fog.
Trying to see what you are looking
for has become quite hard,
As for reading a shopping list,
that's now an impossible task.
Grabbing the nearest thing on the
shelf that resembles what I want,
I appear to have become organic.
On top of that trying to remember
to keep two metres apart,
Remembering I have forgotten the bread,
which is now three aisles back,
Gives me cause to panic.
So I thought I would make it easier
to pop my glasses in the trolley.
So now at least it's just a bit blurry instead.
But it was still blurry on my walk home,
I had left my glasses behind,
My shopping bag on wheels,
which held both milk and wine,

Was now as heavy as lead.
But I turned back to retrieve them.
Luckily the staff at West Vale Tesco
are so friendly and helpful
That I can go back and do it all again,
without being full of dread.

SILENCE

Silence maybe golden,
but some of us find it hard to achieve,
Especially if you find yourself having
songs constantly playing in your head.
At first I thought this was normal so
found it difficult to believe
That not everybody has this,
and that it is known as an ear worm.
Sometimes it is a song that I do not even like,
And I have come to learn that even
the ones I do can wear very thin.
After a whole week, John Martyn's beautiful
"May you never lay your head down without a
hand to hold, and may you never
make your bed out in the cold,"
Ended up annoying me so much
I wished it would take a hike.
Add to this tinnitus, that low constant ringing,
I realise that my chances of hearing
silence has become rather slim.
However, I am lucky that
I can still hear conversations,
Bird song as well as music and the radio,
so this is not a complaint,
Merely an observation.

SIXTY-FIVE

It is hard to believe in just a few days
I will be sixty-five,
Rather than think I am getting old,
I am celebrating the fact I am still alive.
Some days I feel in my body more than others,
But each day I count my blessings,
Especially the privilege of being a
mum and grandmother.
Hence, I will be having a caterpillar cake,
I cannot disappoint my grandson,
It is so that rascal the sweets he can take.
The irony is inside I feel like thirty-five,
Passing shop windows and seeing
the reflection of an older woman,
Then realising it is me.
Looking in the mirror and seeing my mum,
I suppose if I had a fat bank account,
I could choose plastic surgery
or expensive creams,
Wishing these wrinkles were gone.
However, I feel they reflect my
journey through life,
So I do not see why I should be
ashamed of them.
My hope is to collect even more
before my journey is done.

THANK YOU, JAMES VAN PRAAGH

My Christmas present to myself
Was your book *Unfinished Business*,
I have the urge to read every
spiritual book on the shelf.
My search for answers has led me to feel
I have dipped my toe in an ocean,
On how the Universe works,
I still have very little notion.
Like the quest for the Holy Grail,
It's difficult to know where to start.
Am I on the right track or trail?
I need to close my eyes and feel with my heart.
James's book has given me liberation,
The answers I seek are not a million miles away,
For me this is a revelation.
Jesus did say seek and ye will find,
James has expanded on that,
The answers you seek are
deep inside you already,
You only have to quiet your busy mind.

THE FOX AND THE CROW

Walking the dog one windy but dry morning,
Part of the walk was crossing a viaduct where
you really feel that wind blow.
Heading up to an unused road
locally known as Bedlam.
The woods and park were so soggy,
that was my preferred place to go.
As we got further, we reached the place where a
woodland path drops down to the road.
The quiet was then broken by a very noisy crow,
The cawing got stronger as we approached.
It was then that I saw a glimpse of orange and
the white tip of a fox's brush.
It quickly turned tail and
disappeared behind a bush.
Then as we turned around to
make our way back,
The crow cawed twice and then away it flew.
It felt to me, that after the crow
had given out a warning,
The fact we were on our way,
that it already knew.
Then the crow gave the all clear;
it seemed the crow had the fox's back.

THE LONGEST PANTOMIME

So, our traditional pantomime cannot
be held this Christmas,
But fear not, we have two running on together,
both here as well as in the USA.
There will be no audience in the usual way.
President Trump is in the spotlight
and refusing to leave the stage.
He keeps repeating that the
election was a fraud,
Until he hopes the audience
believes what he has to say.
But a baddie called Covid takes centre stage,
to lots of hisses and boos,
You took most of our 2020, now it's 2021 you
are trying to make us lose.
But to loud cheering a fairy godmother appears,
but instead of a wand she is holding A vaccine.
Glad tidings I bring, this will save our nation.
A character called Van Tam then tells us it's
okay, the train is leaving the station.
Then a very weary character crawls on stage,
whose name is Brexit.
It has endured four years of negotiations,
so it is feeling unsteady,
The audience shout, "Fear not, Brexit,
that is behind you, as you are now oven-ready."

However, as it turns out it
might be a difficult exit.
Like Peter Pan, the talks are on the high wire;
we are told it could be deal or no deal,
Hang on, we thought this was a
pantomime instead of a TV show.
But the result hangs on just one meal.
So, this pantomime goes on and on,
longer than a Ken Dodd show.
There will be no loud cheering or a curtain call,
As almost half the population
didn't want it at all.
So, on with the show;
when it stops, nobody knows.

THE NEW PLANET

I saw the new planet again today,
hiding in plain sight.
We are not supposed to notice it;
it is never mentioned in the media,
And we have all been provided
with fascinating devices
At which we have to look down to play.
When the sun disappears behind a cloud
Is when it appears shining,
full and really bright.
I have been told it is the full moon.
How can it be when it is so near
to the sun in the daytime sky?
I would love more people to notice it,
as it is such a new phenomen,Shining there,
so bright and proud.

THE VIRUS

This virus has touched everybody's lives,
In ways we could never imagine in
our wildest dreams.
It has made us feel more global,
as it ignores borders,
Social status and nationality.
We know the future will look different,
As it has taken the world as we know it,
Then ripped it apart by the seams.
We certainly are not the only family
to lose someone dear.
So, our days are not just
different but full of grief.
It makes it far harder when we
have more funerals to attend,
The effects of this virus are far-reaching,
As we realise the duration will not be brief.
My partner did not have Covid,
However, due to poor health, the stress of it
quickened his end, due to fear.
Other people are losing loved ones due to
operations and tests having to be delayed,
So, at the end of this we want to see a nation
who are kinder and more caring.

We have already witnessed some brilliant
inspirers, more creativity,
Along with bravery and lots of lovely sharing.
So, when we come out the other side and
have managed to cope with adversity,
Let's remember all that as well as those we lost,
We deserve a brighter future,
far less selfishness and greed,
Instead let's have much more
understanding and kinder normality.

TURNING AWAY

Sometimes it feels like God or the Universe
has turned its back on us,
Leaving us out in the cold.
This is not true at all;
in fact, it is the reverse.
In times of fear and stress,
the negative energy places us further away.
So, it is ourselves who have turned our backs.
The Universe is pure, unconditional love,
always there,
It's all around us all the time,
Expanding, constant and never growing old.

UNSUNG HEROES

Recently we have heard a lot about the
behaviour of some people who
think only of themselves.
Panic ensued, leaving us in despair
at the sight of empty supermarket shelves.
It feels like the fear of this
pandemic is everywhere,
Questioning our faith in human nature,
as ignorance seems to be all around.
However, it turns out we have thousands of
Earth Angels here with us on the ground,
The doctors and nurses,
paramedics and support staff,
as well as our shop workers and
delivery men too.
Not forgetting the thousands o
f volunteers helping the people
in their community behind the scenes.
None of these unsung heroes are in it for the
glory but simply because they care.

WHAT WE WANT

We all hope that we know what we want,
It's easier to know what material possessions,
But the truth is it is easier
to know what we do not want.
We do not want to be made redundant,
Or illness or death to happen to ourselves,
Or anyone we hold dear.
Therefore, it appears that our
wants are based mostly on fear.
However, the Universe knows
exactly what we need.
It will bring people in our lives that can help us
progress on our journey.
Some situations it brings may feel
like a punishment or a bitter pill.
We may choose to ignore
the coincidences, or synchronicities,
Instead keeping with the status quo,
Too scared to allow any changes, as it feels safer
To keep things the way we already know.
But look back on your life
when your circumstances changed,
Do you remember them as lucky or as a curse?
But it has brought you where
You are right now,
For better or for worse.
But the Universe knows just what you need,
So, try and relax and go with the flow.

WHERE HAVE ALL THE LOO ROLLS AND HAND WASH GONE?

To any of you who are fuelling the shortages,
In order to get your hands on some easy money,
Without a real clue.
If people are desperate
enough to buy your wares,
What did they do when they went to the loo?
Not to mention coughs and sneezes.
I would be checking those tenners if I were you,
Not just for poo, but maybe even
a dose of the Corona flu!

WHY DOES THE FLOOR FEEL FURTHER AWAY?

Why does the floor feel further away?
And steps feel steeper every day.

Looking for my reading glasses
when I pick up a book,
As my eyes have become weak,
Feeling uncomfortable,
as my joints have begun to creak.

No longer looking for love's young dream,
Instead applying the wrinkle cream.

Walking in a room and forgetting why,
No longer running for that bus,
instead letting it pass by.

Asking people to repeat what they have said,
As I have become hard of hearing,
Having to take more breaks
in between the cleaning.

Feeling too hot and then too cold,
as the menopause takes effect,
Again, it's just part of getting old.

This is not a list of lamentations,
But rather as time goes by, mere observations.

I am surrounded by a loving family and friends,
Along with a grandson whom I adore,
So, I feel like a lucky person;
who could ask for anything more?

WHY?????

Boris Johnson, I only have one question
to ask of you and that is, why?
What is it that makes you think
that this country needs
Forty percent more nuclear warheads?
Could it be that now we have left the European
Union you feel we are vulnerable,
That if we were attacked, other countries would
no longer come to our aid?
But it felt safer when we were a part of the non-
proliferation pact.
Now it looks to the rest of the
world as if you are afraid.
How many nuclear warheads
does it take to destroy this planet?
Nowhere near the amount
we already have, and that is a fact.
We will be told that they will keep us safe as a
deterrent, that old argument.
But we believed we already had that:
a nuclear sub called Trident.
The threats now are global, such as this
pandemic, warming and cyber attack.
All the hardware that has been sent up to space.
So, it seems to be yet another poor choice,
That you think it's a good idea to spark off yet
another useless arms race.

WITH YOUR SEATBELTS FASTENED

It has been very difficult to understand
What has been going on in this world.
That something as small as a microbe could
have such a far-reaching effect,
Not just in this country,
but throughout the land.
Flights grounded, movement restricted, people
told to work from home.
In fact, almost limited to our own four walls.
The hardest part being keeping our distance
from family and friends,
When this lockdown will be
over is an unknown.
But for some time now, we have felt we have
been building up for a change to take place.
Time has been speeding up and at times it felt
like the whole world had gone mad.
This could be a part of Mother Earth's shift, but
first she had to get the world's
population To stay in one place.
Just as when we board a plane, there is all the
hustle and bustle of finding your seat,
Stashing your bag and preparing to settle down,
Before the "Fasten your seatbelt" sign comes on.

The gathering speed and then lift off, before
breaking through the clouds,
Into that beautiful azure-blue sky.

Then the boring bit in between before
you land at your destination.
So, our lockdown and Groundhog Days,
may be Mother Earth's seatbelt,
Before we find she has moved to a
more caring and kinder place,
Not just for us but for every nation.

WINTER SOLSTICE

The winter solstice cometh soon,
With winter's icy fingers and
sunsets in the afternoon.
The commercial side of Christmas
is really in full swing,
The pressure of the latest must-have,
Making us forget the joy
simple pleasures can bring.
I miss the simple Christmases
with no batteries to need,
Getting a new book from Santa
and looking forward to the read.

But before I make everyone feel sad,
There are still things that make me feel glad.
My little bird friends coming for their seed,
They dive and swoop and play, putting on a
show, as if to thank me for their feed.

I love the Christmas carols to
remind me of the Nativity,
The getting together of family and friends
To join in the festivity.
But this one will be different from the rest,
I now have a little grandson who smiles and
giggles and fills my heart with joy,
I think this one will be one of the best.

WRONG TURNINGS

I thought I was lucky growing
up in an era of hope,
We thought we could change
the world and had plenty of scope.
We had make love not war, and ban the bomb,
Wearing no makeup and
with our clothes and hair long.
Neil Armstrong on the moon, taking his first
step for mankind,
We were definitely leaving the old world behind.
We decided we needed to open our minds.
Along came the drugs, just a
question of choosing which kind.
Uppers or downers, psychedelic or speed.
Unaware you may end up with
a dangerous habit to feed.
After a time, I realised that
things were getting worse,
The only thing benefiting
was the drug dealer's purse.
Negativity was having a laugh,
Ha-ha, I have sent you down the wrong path.
Then along came technology and materialism,
this is better by far,
Oh good, we can have a new car.

New fridges and freezers and colour TVs,
This is a new world, bring it on, please.
Your fridge has just broken, well, throw it away.
Out with our credit card, get a new one today.
It is important to have the latest designer gear
As quickly as possible while it's still here.
Now you have ended up with a lot of debt,
This has been the best tactic yet.
Negativity was having a laugh,
Ha-ha, I have sent you down the wrong path.
Enlightenment cannot be bought
from a dealer or off the shelf,
But rather it comes from inside yourself.

WEAVERS

The fabric of the Universe is
a sacred living tapestry,
Changing all the time, with multitudes of colour
Along with intricate designs.
These depend on the actions
of the likes of you and me.
The dark colours, knots and snarls
Are caused by trouble and strife.
The beautiful gold and silver threads
Are produced by good thoughts and deeds.
You are all helping to weave
the fabric of the Universe,
As you journey through your life.

SEIZE THE MOMENT

The only thing that matters is today,
Your fretting over the past
and fears about your future
Takes your enjoyment of the here and now
And steals it clean away.
Your money worries we do hear,
The Universe will provide
exactly what you need,
When the time is right.
Your anxiety creates a block,
Making it harder to carry out its deed.
We also hear life is too short,
Or I never have enough time.
But at home you have eternity.
For your contentment, live in the here and now.
Think, today is all I really have.
Seize the moment.
Everything will be fine.

KARMA

Such a little word with so many meanings,
It has become such a part of
your language, and so well used,
People with or without religious leanings,
It is no surprise you get confused.
However, the Universe is not so complicated,
It simply means whatever
thoughts and deeds you send out
Will be returned to you.
Think of it like a roundabout.
When people are in conflict,
You do not need to join in the fight,
It is your own soul you will restrict,
Please try instead to send love and light.

DARE TO DREAM

As you journey along your path in life,
Have faith to hope and dream.
Your ego will race way ahead like a hare,
Placing fear-based obstacles in your way.
It will make it feel like a bumpier ride,
With your dreams too hard to accomplish,
Or so it would it seem.
Please try and brush its nagging doubts aside.
Your spirit has always had the map,
So, like a tortoise what you need are baby steps.
We know your progress may feel slow,
But remember the story of
the tortoise and the hare.
Believe, you already know the way to go,
Slowly but surely, you will get there.

CHURCHES ARE PEOPLE, NOT BUILDINGS

Still Waters Spiritual Centre
closing down so quickly
Came as quite a shock,
But maybe it was a wake-up call,
A time to take stock.
It had taken many years to find,
A whole group of people with a like mind.
This really does feel like a new age,
Materialism has been all the rage.
Drugs, violence and war,
What has that all been for?
All we are doing is wrecking Mother Earth,
Who has been there for us, for every birth.
It is now time to look within,
Not for gadgets but for kith and kin.
We are spirits in human form,
Experiencing for the Universe,
That's why we were born.

SPIRIT GUIDES

I have been given this poem
because I am feeling sad,
I know too many people
who are frightened of giving.
Not to try and help them makes me feel bad,
They are frightened of
death and scared to be living.
They have the comfort of their
spirit guide is all I want to say,
This is really hard, as they
can become angry or upset.
So, the advice I am getting is just to pray.
I have always enjoyed sharing,
Also being told I am too honest or good.
It seems to be in my nature to be caring,
I do not want to change that even if I could.
The Universe, the angels and spirit guides
Give so much love and support,
I want to shout it from
the rooftops for everyone to hear.
But for now they have left me with this thought,
Believe in yourself, pray and have no fear.

STRESS

Stress can change an atmosphere very quick,
Infecting the people around and about,
Making the air around you feel dense and thick,
Causing tempers to flare,
Hurtful remarks to leave the lip,
A bad mood for all that are there,
Any lightness of mood taking a dip.
Stress is part of the human condition,
But allowing negative feelings to grow stronger,
By staying and arguing gives it more validation.
Recognise it and decide you can
bear it no longer,
It's better to remove yourself
from the situation.

LOOKING IN THE
WRONG DIRECTION

Again, the cry goes up to stop immigration,
They are taking our jobs and money,
We want to be one nation.
Please send them back where they belong.
Look to the reasons for these people to leave
their homes and risk all,
They want the same as you,
for their children to know peace,
To escape from oppression, free to stand tall.
Some people die in their flight for freedom.
Light a candle in a dark room,
Now try to stop the moths drawn to the flame.
The answer is simple: light more candles.
These people are no different from you,
Their needs and wants are just the same.
You need to lobby and pray to our world leaders,
Do not build a fortress, but share your gains,
Make the whole world fit to live in.
The large corporations too
need to play their part.
Again, lobby and pray for
them to change their heart.
Pray they lose their money lust,
Or we could all become immigrants,
Looking for another planet,
Our beautiful Earth may
be left nothing but dust.

TAKING FLIGHT

So, your soul wants to lift out,
Free of earthly worries and care.
It wants to dance and sing and shout,
But everyday concerns are always there.
It is hard to put aside time for meditation,
People around you may not understand.
They will ask something of
you without hesitation,
So quickly back to Earth you land.
Please remember that you chose to go back to
the lower vibration,
You went with work to do.
Enjoy short bursts of liberation,
But do not forget your
promise to the Universe too.
Try not to feel empty and down,
Do good and spread the Divine White Light.
Keep that smile and lose that frown,
It will be a short time before once again,
Your spirit can take flight.

TAKE FLIGHT

Looking out of my window and
observing the birds in flight,
I am feeling envious of their
ability to soar above the trees.
Trying to imagine that sensation of freedom,
Which allows them to float upon a breeze.
But back down to Earth,
I have my body to get me around,
Even with feet of clay and
rickety hips and knees.
Watching the swifts as they swoop and dive
catching insects close to the ground.
The stately heron as it
flies backwards and forwards
Looking for fish in the Calder River.
The patterns the rooks make as they form their
own mini murmaration,
The land gulls flying hither and thither.
Smiling as I watch a robin and a blackbird claim
the garden as their territory.
Becoming frustrated by the sparrows which fly
down en masse to do as they please.
They come to take most of the food before
playing aerial tig several times a day.

But when it is my time and my work is done,
I want my spirit to take
off soar, swoop and dive,
Then I can have my own celebration.
Why should the birds have all the fun?

BE THE EYE OF A STORM

With the pandemic, fires, floods,
wars and natural disasters,
It feels like the whole world is on the rampage.
The world is in turmoil and
normal belongs in a different age.
Be witness to these events and try your best to
help one another.
Be the eye in a storm.
What once could remain hidden
is now there for all to see,
Not hiding in plain sight.
All that is rotten and corrupt
is rising to the surface,
Like a boil waiting for that lance.
As difficult as it is to listen to the news,
Try not to allow it to fill you full of dread.
Only bad news attracts the media,
who enjoy giving us a fright.
Staying calm and centred will
allow you to keep a level head.
Be the eye in a storm.
Try to allow your thoughts to
create an area of calm around you,
Switch off the radio and TV and try to meditate.

THOUGHTS

Our thoughts are made up of energy that does
not just remain in our own heads.
Instead, they blend with the universal
energy which is all around us.
The old saying like attracts like is true.
If you are mostly sending out negative thoughts,
Then you are attracting the energies that could
bring you lots of sorrows.
If you can train your mind to
send out more positive thoughts,
Then you are attracting energies
which could lead to happier tomorrows.
This is not easy, as negative
thoughts seem easier for us,
Fears, intolerance, anger, and self-pity.
My own big test recently is
how to cope with grief.
Losing two members of my household,
even if one had four legs instead of two.
I still have to experience the
feelings and allow time to feel sad.
But I keep remembering what
Captain Tom told us,
Tomorrow will be a good
day and send out gratitude.

So, as well as the grief I can appreciate the family and friends I still have here. Hopefully I have more good things to come my way if I keep a positive attitude.

WHAT WE WANT

We all hope that we know what we want.
It is easier with material possessions,
But the truth is we are more certain
of things we don't want.
We do not want anything bad to happen either
to us or to those we hold dear.
So, it appears that our wants are based on fear.
However, the Universe
knows just what we need,
It will bring people and situations into our lives
in order for us to progress.
Sometimes this can feel like bitter
medicine or a punishment,
Or a marvellous opportunity,
the choice being ours to make.
We can ignore these synchronicities, instead
choosing to keep the status quo,
Because it feels safer to hang
onto what we know.
Looking back over your life at times
when circumstances changed,
Does it feel like you were lucky,
or more as a curse?
Either way it has brought you
to where you are now.

If you are wiser and stronger it is the
bad times that allowed you to grow.
The Universe knows just what you need,
so try and relax and go with the flow.

ALL I SEND IS MY ETERNAL LOVE

Your Earth plane is but a school,
You go there to learn your chosen lessons,
So, to aid you in your journey,
I gave you all free will.
So why then would I limit you
with dogma and rules,
That makes no sense at all.
Please do your own research,
Each and every one of you
is precious in my eyes,
To keep misquoting me does my name besmirch.
Yes, you are witnessing the
decline of your church,
But I have not gone away.
I live not just in a building but in your hearts,
At last where I belong.
Repeating words that for you
have very little meaning,
Has really had its day.
I know no feelings of hatred,
damnation and fear,
All I ever send is my eternal love.
Know that all those doctrines
being quoted in your ear,
Are all manmade and do not come from above.
It fills my heart with joy that
for many of you my message
Has come clear.

TRUST

Do not get too complacent,
Again, we will test your faith.
Your trials and tribulations,
May feel Heaven-sent.
But a lot of them your spirit chose,
Before you came.
If times were always good,
What would you have to learn?
Your soul's bravery and intent,
Would not be put to their best use.
So, learn to trust and meditate,
Pray and stand firm.
It is when times are troubled
That we find our true strength.
In our human form
It's easy to worry and doubt,
But with faith and trust,
All your fears you can overturn.

SAT NAV

Your flesh-and-blood body is
just the vehicle your soul chose
In order to experience a human
life on the denser Earth plane.
Of this your soul and higher self knows,
But due to the amnesia with each life,
you forget just the same.
We know it is not easy but try not
to allow your ego into the driver's seat,
It is far better to allow your soul to
guide you to your destination,
It is your inbuilt sat nav.
With our help you already planned your route,
This way it will be far easier to come
home to us with your lessons complete.

THE OLD SCHOOL YARD

You will be finding your
development can set you apart,
It may feel you are back in that old school yard.
It is simply you are looking at a bigger picture
With less ego and more heart.
The petty squabbles over very little at all,
When they reach your ears, make you
think you cannot be bothered.
It is not because you are superior,
It is because you are standing tall.
You may also feel sad about the greedy
nature of some people around you,
Try not to get upset and annoyed.
As you are aware you already have it all.
All they have will turn to dust.
It may be that they are a young
soul with less experience.
It may be that your own soul is
older and more mature.

LOVE AND LIGHT

We see your daily struggle
when someone has upset you,
Bad thoughts about that person
slip easily into your brain.
You have learned that your thoughts are real,
The bad feelings will be sent to that person,
Faster than an express train.
We prefer you instead to send love and light,
This lessens the harm your thoughts can do.
We know some days feel like an uphill fight,
But they help block the bad thoughts,
Allowing the good ones through.
It is not what you say or think on the outside,
But behind those, the intention.
Your thinking is quite correct,
Sending love and light through gritted teeth,
Really has no effect.
Your intentions to us are as clear as day,
Are your thoughts for the greater good,
or just self-serving?
The soft, sweet words, some people say,
Is the intention for your good,
or is it manipulation?
For your sanity amongst an earthly population,
Just send love and light.

THANK YOU TO ALL OF MOTHER NATURE'S CARING ARMY

For people who we see in their
hearts selfishness and greed,
You are a namby-pamby do-gooder,
Of nature's gifts and beauty they have no need.
We see you who have the bigger picture
Have the wisdom and are smart.
They are blinkered and only
look for profit and gain,
Your views to them are a threat,
as they have more to lose.
They see growth as a runaway train.
For years they have shouted the loudest,
to drown you out,
But they have not succeeded yet.
They tell you big corporations
are for the benefit of all,
However, that has not been your experience,
You can see through their lies so tall.
They will make even more of you poor,
so they can give you less.
They will turn Mother Nature into a concrete
jungle, or a wasteland.
Then tell you it is in the name of progress.
You are a strong, caring person of Mother
Nature's caring army,
We thank you, and on each
of your heads do bless.

ME, MYSELF AND I

Me, myself and I is a lonely path to tread,
You may feel the need for attention,
And may disappear inside your own head.
We understand it is part of the human state,
Your ills and woes are too numerous to mention,
We often hear the cry of "Why me?"
as you berate.
The key to unlocking this isolation
is to think of others,
You are a thread in a large tapestry.
It's good to spend time in contemplation,
But you need to remember to be brotherly.
Sadly, we witness the "poor me"
thinking leading to bitterness and bile,
Our purpose of being on Mother Earth is to give
each other a helping hand.
It is much easier to be around
people who make you smile,
If you put aside your ego, happiness could
spread throughout the land.

KEEP YOUR SPIRITS HIGHER

Well done, you have tuned
into the universal energy,
Your path may be strewn with
rocks and seems like a mire.
But your journey will be smoother
when you lift your spirits higher.
For your path leads forever onwards,
no chance of turning back,
When everyday worries and
stress become just an annoyance,
You are keeping on the right track.
On your plane negativity abounds,
Life may hand you a poisoned chalice,
It is your choice if you drink from this cup.
It is full of sorrow, spite, greed and malice.
Keep your spirits high and from
this there is no need to sup.
The contents lead to loneliness,
depression and despair.
Try and help those people,
but from your own path do not waver,
Your thoughts and feelings
they do not understand.
They may say you are mad or
deluded or use other ploys.

Keep moving along your way,
fulfil your job in hand,
For you these slings and arrows
are but children's toys.

THE UNITY OF RELIGION

I am looking forward to the
day when all religions unite,
It is simply different paths
leading to the same plane.
I feel so sad to see fellow humans fight,
But to do it in my name
causes me even more pain.
Every religion has its place,
one no better than another.
I am known by many different names,
but always the same face.
When you think of me, think of the
tenderness shown to a baby by its mother.

A LITTLE COMFORT FOR
THE LOSS OF A PET

To all of you heartbroken
from losing a beloved pet,
We send you extra blessings and love.
We understand they were a family member,
So can cause you a lot of grief.
There is a special place
here for your pets to reside,
We know no time, so for
them your parting will be brief.
When the day arrives and it
is time for you to go home,
A signal goes out to all your loved ones,
the same place to come.
They form a welcoming party just for you,
A time of celebration is to be had,
It is your beautiful animal friends
that push to the front of the queue.

FEAR

The age of Aquarius is a new day dawning,
As the Earth moves nearer to a higher vibration
It heralds the end of the old order,
Into a new morning.
The big corporations and mass media
Are the ones who have truly
been running the show.
They are behind all the wars and disorder,
Much more than you have been led to know.
The dark forces have also joined together,
They spread fear, as that is their food and drink.
As the new day dawns they
will try and have the final say.
So please stay strong and let your light shine,
Try to keep away the fear
and get on with your day.
This way it will be a far better
future for yours and mine.

KEEP THE FAITH AND ASK

I am both your mother and father,
Many of you know me by a different name.
I love you all in a way you cannot imagine,
Each and every one of you is
precious to me just the same.
As a loving parent I want to
give each of you what you need.
I see you at times running around
like a chicken without a head,
Please try and control your ego,
stop, slow down and take heed.
Why all this stress and panic?
You could talk to me instead.
I know at times for some of you,
life seems a heavy task,
It is easy to lose your faith when times are bad,
But you should know all you have to do is ASK.
I am waiting to make your life smoother
In order to carry out your purpose.
Help pay your bills and keep you out of debt.
So please remember you
have everything to gain,
Keep the faith, you ain't seen nothing yet.

UNLEASH YOUR INNER GODDESS

The age of Aquarius heralds
the rise of the Goddess.
Along with people becoming more spiritual.
The age of Pisces was the age
of patriarchy and materialism.
Power is never easily given up, so Pisces will not
just give in without a fight.
But the old ways of exerting dominance are
slowly beginning to unwind.
This is completely different from
Women's Lib in the seventies.
This involved either man
hating or copying male behaviour.
This is more about accepting each other's
differences and being respectful and kind.
This is for the benefit of both men and women,
like Yin and Yang coming together,
Accepting we are equals is the way forward into
a future which is far more bright.
So, let us all release our inner Goddess.

AMERICAN DREAM

America, as a teenager I looked to you,
You were setting a flame alight.
Of your hippy movement I was in awe,
Offering us California dreaming, flower power,
Not forgetting make love not war.

You also gave us singer-song-writers
who were poets and rebels,
Trend-setters to the world.
A real hope of peace and love,
Pop festivals which were full of fun.
President Kennedy, a real breath of fresh air,
Not only handsome, he could put
a man on the moon.
We were so excited about your
future and what was to come.

As an older woman I look to you to see a flame
burning far dimmer.
The hopes and dreams dashed,
Instead of flower power there
are even more powerful drugs,
As the idea of peace grows even slimmer.
Instead of pop festivals you worship the gun.
You are now as polarised as us,
fear and hatred are rife.

So, any hope for a brighter future
feels like swimming upstream.
But I never want to lose all hope in humanity,
If you want to come together
and rekindle that flame,
Put aside your differences,
decide you have had enough,
Instead of the misery choose
to look for a better life.
Not just for you but the rest of the world,
do not let the flame go out.
Let's try to remember the American dream.

MONEY IS NOT MY MASTER

Money is not my master,
In fact it brings forth too much greed.
Having enough to be comfortable,
have holidays and help other people
Is all I really need.
Material things bring a passing pleasure,
You could horde a lot of money,
diamonds and gold,
But you cannot take it with you
when you shake off this mortal coil.
Unconditional love is where real joy lies,
And that could never be bought or sold.

THE PEN IS MIGHTIER
THAN THE SWORD

It is true that the pen is
mightier than the sword,
Everybody should have
the right to an education.
Being able to read and write
as well as the spoken word.
People who want power by
keeping other people in ignorance
Shows they are not real leaders or they would
not have to stoop to corruption,
They know that citizens who are literate are
more capable of making their own decisions,
Making it harder for them to influence.
I went to a secondary modern Catholic school,
Possibly not the best education.
However, what it did was to
give me the grounding and tools
To continue educating myself,
not just achieving a DipHE
But being able to think for myself.

ANIMAL LOVERS

It is not easy for animal lovers to
witness the cruelty which goes on,
It is really difficult to imagine how
some people can be so heartless and cruel.
It makes a caring person want to
put their head in their hands in weeping.
It makes no difference if they are
wild animals, farm animals or pets.
The instinct is to wrap them up in
our arms for their own safekeeping.

But as well as praying for
animals safe-keeping,
It is important to say a prayer
for the perpetrators too,
Even though it is them we despise.
It may help them to become less
heartless and brutal and ignorant.
They are lacking the very emotions
which define us as being human beings,
In the hope it may open some of their eyes.

All animals need is places to live,
food resources and our respect.
They demand nothing from us
but to be left alone or loved,
So, let's hope those so-called humans
who hurt and kill for fun
Move higher up in our evolution,
before the animals are extinct.

THREE CHEERS FOR SPRING

It is the time of year when you
feel spring in the air,
The sun climbing higher in the sky,
Allowing us to feel the heat from its rays,
Sensing the sap rising in the trees,
Seeing the new shoots pushing
up from the Earth,
The relief of having longer days.

Being able to leave the house
without being all bundled up,
Leaving behind those gloves and boots,
Being able to throw open
the windows and doors,
Blow away the winter blues and cobwebs,
Looking forward to enjoying the outdoors,
So let's celebrate 21st March, a very special day.

THE TREES

In this poem I would like to pay homage
to that wonder of nature, the trees,
I have been blessed to walk amongst
them for the last fifty-five years.
I feel a part of them as well as they are
part of me.
They have been a constant in my life,
always there,
No matter how I am feeling.
They know all my secrets, my worries and fears.
Amongst them I feel safe,
as they always give me healing.
As I walk or sit amongst them, their calm
presence always dries any tears,
Or just out feeling happy and enjoying the walk.
Some of them are quite old and
have weathered many a storm,
What changes have they been witness to?
I so wish my language they could talk.
It is the fact that they were
here before I was born,
After I am gone they will still stand,
That makes my problems feel quite small.
So, I wish to say a big thank
you to these majestic trees,

Always there when I need a helping hand,
Being an example of staying calm
and standing proud and tall,
For I feel a part of them, as well
as they are a part of me.

AN HONOURED GUEST

You have been invited as an honoured guest
To a beautiful home,
Where everything you could
possibly want is laid out on her table.
Would you not choose your
behaviour which is best?
After all her welcome has been bar none.

Would you feel free to walk in
and wreck her beautiful place,
then steal whatever you think worth taking?
Showing her complete contempt and disrespect,
with no honour in the making.

So why do so many of you
think it is perfectly fine
To treat our planet Earth like this.
Without her gifts you would have nothing.
She provides all our basic needs as well as
bounties such as honey and wine.
Her gifts are meant for everyone,
not just a so-called chosen few.

GUT INSTINCT

On the whole, human beings
are sociable animals,
Enjoying the company of others.
We may be looking for that one
person who makes our heart sing.
It is a godsend if you both want the same thing.
Problems arise when you both
have different agendas,
Maybe you are wanting commitment and they
just want you to be lovers.
It is really special if you are part of a family or
relationship which is caring
And being able to experience
unconditional love.
Where the opposite exists,
much heartache that can bring.
At times we all enjoy our own company
and look forward to some space.
However, too much time in solitude can lead to
loneliness and depression,
Leaving you in a really bad place.
In the presence of some people you may
Feel uncomfortable for no apparent reason,
Giving you confusing feelings
of the need to back away.

While on the other hand you may meet a
stranger who feels so familiar,
It is difficult to believe you only met that day.
Occasionally you may come across a narcissist;
they are really friendly and charming,
They seem so interested in you
and come across very caring,
Working really hard to lure you into ignoring
your own gut instinct, they are so disarming.
They can be a new boyfriend,
friend or workmate, male or female.
Given time their intentions
will become more clear,
It is to control every aspect of your life; they are
the only one who knows best.
They slowly chip away at your self-esteem, tell
you you are stupid and you
have yourself To blame.
Making you question your own
judgement because their actions,
Fly in the face of everything you hold dear.
Especially if this situation leads to violence, it is
you as the victim who feels the shame.
Do not waste any more time on this person;
pack a bag and run the other way.

They will be angry, not wanting you to go, but
this is about them not wanting to lose control,
Do not listen to any more of their lies; simply
walk away and if you have to, lay low.
Slowly your self-esteem will return and you will
feel stronger because you managed to
Pull yourself away from their clutches and face a
brand new day without the fear.

ON OR OFF

We are ending up with a lot
more electrical devices
Which need charging up regularly.
I myself can now add e-cigs to my list,
Along with the mobile phone and laptop.
It is so frustrating when you want to use it
To find the charging bit you missed.
The thought flitted through my mind
The other day when feeling low,
I wish I could plug myself
into the National Grid,
Maybe I would give myself
a boost and a glow.
Then I realised it is not
switching on I need, but off.
My mind is full of constant
chatter the whole time I am awake,
I need to try to meditate more,
calm down these thoughts,
It is time to give myself a break.
This is never easy, as your mind
does not want to be given time out,
But I try to concentrate on soothing music,
to give it something to do.
This is the best way to relax,
of this I have no doubt.

HISTORY

In the early 1960s I was sitting
at my desk in primary school
When the teacher showed us a map of the world.
She then produced a long rule
and pointed out our tiny island.
Britain was coloured pink.
She then showed us lots of other countries,
some really large also coloured pink.
She told us that our tiny island
ruled over the other pink ones.
She also told us that we should all be proud.
Looking at the map I was confused;
how could this be?
However, we could still feel the
sting of a ruler or blackboard duster,
So I kept it to myself, not daring to ask out loud.
I thought about it for a while but
it still remained a mystery.
So, I took myself off to our local
library and found the history shelf,
I would have to satisfy my curiosity for myself.
I found it uncomfortable reading,
beginning to wish I had never started.
The more I found out I became
more heavy-hearted.

It was finding out this country formed
a slave triangle along with America,
Now instead of pride I felt nothing but shame.
But I have had to try and reconcile the fact that
this was done by our ancestors.
It was too heavy a burden for
me to take any blame.
So now I feel neither proud nor
ashamed that I was born here,
My main feeling now is that I am grateful.

SUPER POWER

Who is that old woman in the mirror,
Considering the eyes looking
back at me are mine?
It must be me.
Going about my business I sometimes forget,
Even though my body is rickety,
Inside I still think I am forty.
The most annoying thing for
me was being out and about,
And being ignored, especially in shops.
It felt like I was wearing a cloak of invisibility.
But now I look on it as my new super power.
I can wear what I want, not having to follow
fashion or conventionality.
I can dress like a hippy again, with lots of
colours, cheesecloths and velvets.
Remembering the time of flower power,
Without the platform shoes though, instead red
Kicker boots and sparkly Doc Martens.
My super power allows me this ability.
No facelift or Botox for me,
Yes, my face does reflect back
a woman almost seventy,
With all the experiences in
the wrinkles and laughter lines,
But scratch the surface and there still lurks a
woman who thinks she's forty.

EIN HERZ FÜR AUTOREN A HEART FOR AUTHORS À L'ÉCOUTE DES AUTEURS MIA ΚΑΡΔ
 RTA FÖR FÖRFATTARE UN CORAZÓN POR LOS AUTORES YAZARLARIMIZA GÖNÜL
ORE PER AUTORI ET HJERTE FOR FORFATTERE EEN HART VOOR SCHRIJVERS TEM
ZÖINKÉRT SERCE DLA AUTORÓW EIN HERZ FÜR AUTOREN A HEART FOR AUTHO
RAÇÃO ВСЕЙ ДУШОЙ К АВТОРАМ ETT HJÄRTA FÖR FÖRFATTARE Á LA ESCUCHA DE
EURS MIA ΚΑΡΔΙΑ ΓΙΑ ΣΥΓΓΡΑΦΕΙΣ UN CUORE PER AUTORI ET HJERTE FOR FORFA
AZARLARIMI ZÖINKÉRT SERCE DLA AUTORÓW E
OR SCHRIJVE OS RAÇÃO ВСЕЙ ДУШОЙ К АВТОРАМ ETT

The author

Christine Stretton was brought up as a Catholic
in Halifax, West Yorkshire, where she still lives. At
the age of fifteen, Christine began a hairdressing
apprenticeship but soon decided that neither this
vocation nor religion were her true calling. Later
in life, however, Christine began reading about
Buddhism and Sufism and developed an interest
in meditation and psychic spiritualism. It was at
this point that Christine began penning poetry,
a hobby which flourished and culminated in the
publishing of her work. She has also trained to
become a qualified reiki practitioner.

Christine is sixty-nine years old, the mother of
two children and grandmother to a nine-year-old
grandson. She has lived alone with her dog, Boo
Boo, since her partner, Stuart, died in 2020.

The publisher

He who stops
getting better
stops being good.